IF I HAD
KNOWN

LIFE LESSONS FROM AN OLYMPIC PRO ATHLETE

JONATHAN HORTON

PUBLISHING GROUP

ISBN - 9781790123124

Book layout design & eBook conversion by manuscript2ebook.com

 A Ninja Coalition Book

PRAISE FOR *IF I HAD KNOWN*

This book describes what it takes to get to the top of a sport and how much work and dedication it takes. It shows what it takes to be an Olympic gymnast and the sacrifices you need to make. But that's not all. It teaches anybody who wants something to push themselves as far as they can, to believe in themselves and to recognize that they can achieve great things. This is a great read for anyone looking for motivation or for anyone wanting to see what it takes to be one of the best in the world.

-Jake Dalton
Member of the U.S. National Team
4 X World Medalist
2012 & 2016 Olympian

TABLE OF CONTENTS

INTRODUCTION

My name is Jonathan Horton, and I am a two-time Olympic gymnast. At the 2008 Olympic games in Beijing, China, I won both a silver and a bronze medal. In 2012, I became the captain of the Olympic team, and my plan was to compete in the 2016 Olympic games as well. Unfortunately, I ruptured my rotator cuff nine months before I would have a shot at my final Olympic Games. At the age of 32, I retired from my sport after giving gymnastics every ounce of effort that I possibly could. Fortunately, I can walk away from my career knowing that I gave it my all, and I have zero regrets.

I know this sounds ridiculous, but I got my start in the sport at the ripe young age of four. It came about because of a funny situation that I got myself into while shopping with my parents at Target. While their backs were both turned the other way, I scampered up a 25-foot support beam and made it all the way to the ceiling in no time! My parents were completely astonished and figured that I probably had some kind of freakish talent, and in order to develop it, they enrolled me in a gymnastics class.

Truthfully? I wasn't the most talented kid in the world. I wasn't the strongest, I wasn't the fastest, and I have always been a super slow learner. What I did have was a ton of energy, and I was fearless!

I started competing at the age of six. At that time, I wasn't what most people would think of as an "Olympian." I wasn't an instant success, or a child prodigy. I walked away from countless competitions with nothing to show; no medals, no ribbons, no trophies.

However, in 1996, at the age of eleven, everything changed for me. I watched my first Olympic Games! When I saw the greatest athletes in the world win medals for their country, I knew I wanted to do the same thing.

After the Olympics ended that year, I knew my "why." I was completely inspired and wanted to experience the same things those athletes had experienced. In fact, the desire was so intense that I felt as if there was no way I could live without knowing that I tried to become an Olympian.

As a kid who wasn't the most talented, I was faced with a lot of obstacles; not only physical challenges, but mental ones, too. People told me that it would be impossible for me to be an Olympian. I wasn't strong enough, flexible enough, or naturally gifted enough. Even when I proved people wrong and became one of the best gymnasts in the world, there were naysayers who were vocal about doubting me.

After my first Olympics in 2008, the story of what my team and I accomplished was impactful worldwide because it came after years of adversity.

The Olympics in 2004 had been a huge success for the United States Gymnastics team. That team won Team USA's first medal, a silver, since 1984, and Paul Hamm won gold in the all-around. Everyone left the games with shiny medals and the team was hailed as one of the greatest ever; just second behind the 1984 team that won gold. Paul Hamm was the first American to ever win the individual all-around title, and the team was massively celebrated! But after the 2004 Olympics was over, Paul and his twin brother Morgan retired, and so did the rest of the entire 2004 team. USA men's gymnastics was left without any experience or leaders to help the next generation of upcoming Olympic hopefuls.

To say that the new group struggled would be an understatement. Zero medals were won in 2005 at the World Championships, one bronze medal was awarded in 2006, but the team placed 13th (the worst finish in history), and in 2007, the US men's gymnastics team placed 4th on five separate occasions; still leaving the World Championships without a medal. As the 2008 games approached, it wasn't a surprise that nobody believed in the ability of the US men's gymnastics program.

In spite of all we were up against in 2008, we left the Beijing Olympics with two medals: a bronze medal in the team competition and a silver that I received on high-bar. The performance of the American team was such a shock that the television networks weren't even planning to air our competition. It wasn't until our team was sitting in first place after the first several rotations of competition that the media started paying attention. We had them on their toes until the bitter end! We caught fire at the Olympics, and it was pretty special; but even though we had accomplished so much, the naysayers immediately attributed our success to nothing but luck. They also had some theories about me.

I had just competed at my first Olympics. I was twenty-two years old. And the critics told me that for the London Olympics, four years away, I would be too old and out of my prime.

Others refused to believe that I could be a consistent "go-to" leader that would encourage the team to continue to thrive—and these are just some examples of what I heard.

I had heard all of the doubters and their discouraging words at every level of my career, but I made a very intentional decision to ignore them. You see, I knew they couldn't understand my work ethic, my desire to succeed, or my team of people I had in my corner.

In the end, I accomplished my goals—but I didn't do it alone and it certainly wasn't easy. I had to dig deeper every step of the way, and during my journey, I learned a lot about perseverance and what it takes to be successful.

Over the years, I've been fortunate enough to work with some of the best of the best, not only in my sport, but in nutrition, sports psychology, and business. I've written this book because I want to share the knowledge that I have gained with the next generation of hard-working athletes, entrepreneurs, doctors, lawyers, or any others who have a big dream. I can't help imagining what I could have accomplished 'if I had known' what I know now many years before taking this journey.

I've had the privilege of soaking in the highest of highs, and sulking at the lowest of lows. From leading Team USA to the worst performance in international history, to standing on the medal podium at the Olympic games with two medals, I've experienced just about every up and down you can imagine at the elite level of a sport. What I have found to be the greatest experience of my career is not the end result of becoming an Olympian, but rather the entire journey that took me there.

One of my passions is to share my unique story and all the knowledge that I gained about life along the way.

Although I have written this book primarily for aspiring elite and professional athletes, I do believe that there is valuable information in it for anyone who hopes to become a high achiever.

Is that you? Do you aspire to be great in your sport, career, or life?

Then let's go!

Chapter 1

STOP TRYING TO BE COOL

Having the ability and opportunity to impact others' lives is one of my greatest passions! Today I do that by speaking around the country, and it's something I love to do.

I once visited a middle school in Southern California to speak, and in the middle of my presentation, I was forced to stop. In the back of the room was a group of chair-slouching guys who wouldn't stop laughing and talking. They all had their phones out, and weren't paying attention at all. I continued speaking for a while, until I was completely fed up with the disrespect.

I stopped what I was doing and said, "Hey! Guys in the back! What's up?"

I tried my best to be polite and almost funny, but I honestly wasn't sure where this interaction would go. Not one of them responded back, but they froze. The entire auditorium was silent.

I took a good look at them and said, "You guys look athletic. Do any of you play sports?"

One of them looked up, and with a condescending grin on his face, he said, "Yeah, we are the football team."

I said, "Sweet! Do you guys love playing the game?"

A couple of them gave me a little nod, some of them laughed, and a few of them shook their heads. I stood there for a second, nodding my head at them, and smiling like I was excited to have our little chat. Finally, I said, "Fellas, I'm going to give you a little advice. This one's on me, and it's totally free. You guys are all way too cool. I don't even know why I'm up here. Each of you is so awesome that you should be up here sharing what it takes to be successful as a professional athlete. I'm sure every one of you are NFL-bound."

I stopped for a second, and I could see the looks of concern on the teachers' and administrators' faces. Trust me, I got nervous for a second, but I continued.

"Guys, I know you want to laugh, joke, be cool and pretend like the guy on stage is a waste of your time. I know that it's way more fun to act like school is worthless, play on your phones, and try to act like you're 'the man' because you have what it takes to be disrespectful to your teachers, coaches, and the speaker who is doing his best to help you be successful. Here's the deal, though—you guys may like to act cool, but I have seen a whole bunch of people in my life who had way more talent than I do, 'cool' themselves all the way to NOTHING."

At this point, I wish I had a video of every single teacher smiling and clapping all at once. I finished up my little rant by telling the kids that what would be cool is to study hard, listen to sound advice that came their way, become obsessed with their career and athletic goals, and do something big with their lives. Sure, they may be called "lame," "teacher's pet," or whatever else comes with being a committed human being, but the last laugh would go to the person standing at the top. Every one of them sat up in their chairs and listened to every word that came out of my mouth for the next 30 minutes.

I was terrified to stop my program at that moment, but it changed my perspective and I'm glad I did it. I realized during my tangent just how extremely kids are pressured to try to fit in. Whether they want to or not, a lot of them put on a different persona in front of their friends that isn't even who they truly are. I hope, at that moment on stage, I was able to change the mindset of one of those students. Even if it was just one, that would be enough for me.

One of the hardest things to do in life is to block out what everyone else is doing and focus on our own goals. I remember being in middle school and high school, where everyone had to have a certain kind of clothes, had to say certain things, or be perceived a certain way to fit in with the crowd. If you didn't do/say/wear what was trending at the time, you weren't cool, and you ran the risk of people making fun of you.

Nothing has changed today. I go to hundreds of schools every year to share the story of my journey to becoming an Olympian, and I continue to see kids who think they are so cool that they can be disrespectful, lazy, and bullies to others. There are always the kids in the back of the room who are being disruptive by making jokes, or poking fun at the speaker on stage just to get laughs out of the students around them. There is always the star athlete who thinks he will become a multi-million-dollar professional one day, who feels that he doesn't need to listen because he has life all figured out.

At the highest level of anything, the people with the biggest dreams, most intense work ethic, and greatest ability to shut everything else out and focus, are the ones who will succeed. These personality traits and abilities have to be intentionally developed from a young age.

This is not an easy thing to do! I promise you, I get it. You want to fit in. You want to go out with friends. You want to crack jokes and act like school is boring, training hard is lame and you don't really care that much.

But let's be honest- you're lying to yourself. You may not love school, but you know it's important to work hard and potentially earn a scholarship one day. You know you need to grind out a good workout every day in training to reach the pinnacle of your sport. If you don't desire those results, well, you may need to reconsider what you're putting your mind and body through.

But if you DO desire those results, you need to let the people around you hate on you a little bit. Let them give you a hard time for being different, if that's what's cool to them and makes them feel good. Let them tell you that you're too obsessed with your dreams or try to convince you that those dreams won't come true and you shouldn't even try. Let them make fun of you for studying hard, being a respectful student, and for trying to grow as a leader.

Not much changes in the real world after your school career is in the rearview mirror. There will always be the people who are too cool to put in long hours, too cool to fully commit to anything, and too cool to step out of their own comfort zone of laziness.

While you are out accomplishing greatness because of your commitment, you will have "friends" who look back in a few years and wish that they had taken things a little more seriously and not tried to be so "cool."

Chapter 2

LET THE HATERS WIN

As far as gymnastics is concerned, I was not the most naturally-gifted kid. I really struggled with a lot of the typical skills that kids were learning, and I had to get creative with my style. I struggled with being able to do a lot of intricate skills, and I started developing routines that weren't the most traditional in style. But hey, it's what I was good at! I found myself doing more high flying and risky skills that took a lot of guts to try, versus the very technical ones. I had people tell me immediately, "That plan will never work - it's too risky. You can't do a routine like that because no one's ever succeeded that way."

As I advanced through the sport, nothing really changed. I was always the guy who did the risky sets.

I wasn't the most stylish and traditionally-appealing gymnast, and despite trying my best, I just wasn't meant to be what the sport was usually looking for. It took me a long time to find my identity, and during those times of searching, I heard a lot of people's opinions about me and what they thought the outcome of my career was going to be.

I heard comments like these:

- "If you keep doing that you will max out before college."

- "No way that skill will work if you keep doing it like that."

- "If you do that routine it'll never work in competition."

- "You need to fix your style because the judges will never accept it."

- "Your gymnastic style doesn't appropriately represent the United States."

Yeah, someone actually said that last statement to my face.

More often than I can count, I had people tell me that it was going to be too hard to make it to the Olympic Games. It would have been really easy to argue with the people that made all of these statements. In fact, when I look back on it, I probably did argue with them a lot, and it gave them the satisfaction of knowing that they got under my skin. Ultimately, it got me nowhere.

One thing I've learned as I've gotten older is to just let people say what they want to say. Let them get it off their chests. It's something that they're worried about, not me! I had so many competitors, coaches, and others who thought they knew what they were talking about—but they didn't understand my drive and my passion. Only I could feel that! There were people who told me I couldn't do something they couldn't even do themselves.

I always thought, "Why would I ever listen to them if they have no idea what it takes?"

Would you take financial advice from someone who is not wealthy? Take fitness advice from someone who isn't fit? Take parenting advice from someone who doesn't have kids?

Simply put, I say let the haters win! Let them have the satisfaction of thinking that they know what's right, that they know what's going to happen, that they know the outcome, and brush it off. Keep moving forward! For me, I have found so much more satisfaction when I'm simply doing what I am meant to do and not trying to prove anything to anyone else except myself. Sure - from time to time, proving the haters wrong did feel pretty good. In the end, though, what felt best was to just let them say what they wanted to say. To let them pretend that they were right, then go do what they said was impossible without even acknowledging their opinion.

There are going to be a lot of people in your life who think that they know what you are capable of. People who think that they know your potential, or people who think they know more than you do.

Hear me loud and clear! The only person who is in control of what you are capable of, the only person who has the ability to create success in your life, is you. No one else has the ability to control your destiny unless you let them.

When I think about this idea of shaking off the naysayers and pressing forward, I think about other athletes like Steph Curry, the star basketball player with the Golden State Warriors. When he was drafted into the NBA, his scouting report tore him apart and declared him not ready for the NBA. Now he's a multiple time NBA world champion and MVP.

I think about NCAA football star and NFL quarterback Tim Tebow, who at every level of the game of football was told his mechanics weren't right, and that he would never be a winner. He became a state champion, an NCAA national champion, and he won two playoff games in the NFL against teams that people said were impossible for him to beat.

I even think about an outstanding athlete like Lebron James, one of the greatest basketball players ever, who has won many games and gone to eight final appearances in a row. People are still tearing him down, hating on him and his ability. He could let it get to him, or he could push through and continue to prove why he's potentially the greatest of all time.

Let the haters win and let them think that they're right. Turn the other cheek and keep moving forward. At the end of the day, only one side's opinion will prove to be right; yours or theirs.

Who will it be?

Chapter 3

GETTING INTO COLLEGE

Although I want my stories in this book to be applicable to anyone, I have it on my heart to share with my readers what my college decision making process was like. Deciding on a university was one of the toughest decisions I had to make and a lot of factors went into my final pick. As I speak with junior high and high school students regularly, I have found that so many of them are lost, scared, have very little guidance, and have no idea what is important when it comes to making the right choice. I hope my college experiences can help ease some of the strain!

When I was in 8th grade and my teachers began talking about college, it felt like a million years away. I didn't want to think about it! Of course, the next four years of high school flew by, and before I knew it, I had to choose a school.

I took a good look at three different universities with Division 1 gymnastics: The University of Michigan, The University of Oklahoma, and Penn State. I was excited about the potential I saw in all three! I had been keeping up with NCAA men's gymnastics for a while, and there were a lot of gymnasts that I really looked up to on every team.

I was offered recruiting trips to all three, and decided to start with Michigan. As soon as I stepped on campus, I fell in love with the University. The team, the coaches, the school, and the football were awesome! When I returned home, I immediately began filling out the application to become a Michigan Wolverine.

A week later, I took my second recruiting trip to Penn State. After this trip, I was 100% convinced that I was going to become a Penn State Nittany Lion. I had more fun in two days at Penn State than I had ever had in my young life. I got to hang out with the team, stay on campus in the dorms, go to an amazing football game, and watch the guys practice in an incredible gymnastics facility. I told myself that there was no way I would pick anywhere else other than Penn State.

Although I had made up my mind on what college to attend, I took my third recruiting trip to the University of Oklahoma for thoroughness' sake. Let's just say I wasn't swayed one bit after my trip to Oklahoma! I was going to Penn State—at least I thought I was. But I just didn't feel the same connection at Oklahoma. The team was great, the coaches were some of the best in the country, and the University was beautiful, but I just felt like Penn State was the place for me.

I went home and told my parents that I had made up my mind to go to Penn State. Since my whole family lived in Houston, Texas (located a short six-hour drive from Oklahoma), this decision didn't go over very well. My mom and dad didn't love the idea of me being more than a quick drive away from home. They wanted to be able to see me from time to time and keep up with my gymnastics as best as they could.

I battled different scenarios in my head for days. Oklahoma didn't feel quite right, but it made sense for my family. Penn State felt like home, but I knew I would never get to see my home-town friends or family.

In the end, after a little bit of begging from my parents, I somewhat reluctantly chose Oklahoma.

Best. Decision. Ever.

Although my choice didn't make as much sense for me at the time, when I stepped on campus to move in, met all of my new teammates, started going to class and began training, everything fell into place. Oklahoma became my home, and my friends and teammates became family. It wasn't love at first sight, but it became clear in a matter of days that I had made the right decision.

I think I could have been pretty happy at any school, but I made that decision based on more than just myself and what felt right for me. I made my decision based on family, gymnastics, and a bit of a "wing it" mentality.

I encourage you to find a school where you know you can grow—not only as a person, but as a student and an athlete. I experienced an incredible season of growth during my collegiate years, but that growth wasn't always easy! Waking up early for work outs, going to class, working out again, attending more classes, studying for exams, writing papers, and striving to be an elite athlete were all challenging activities. But, I grew into the person I am today because of and through those experiences. This may not be a popular opinion, but I don't think college is just about getting smarter or learning about a particular career choice. College is a time to find out what you're really made of, find out what you want to be made of, decide what is important to you, discover your true work ethic, and become an independent capable individual.

Picking the right school is tough, but realistically, it is kind of hard to choose a bad major university these days. They all have amazing professors, athletic programs, campuses, and more. The question is, what feels right for not only you, but your family, and your future?

I chose Oklahoma, and after four years of incredibly hard work, I got to call myself an NCAA National Champion, All-American, college graduate, and most importantly, lifelong friend to some of the greatest teammates on the planet.

Chapter 4

SEPARATE YOURSELF FROM THE OTHERS

- Be respectful
- Have integrity
- Put others' feelings before your own
- Stand up and shake hands firmly when meeting someone
- Look people in the eye when they are talking to you
- Make "sir" and "ma'am" a regular part of your vocabulary
- Remember people's names
- Show gratitude with a genuine "Thank you"
- Speak the truth with confidence and be direct
- Remember that your actions always speak louder than your words

I have junior high and high school athletes ask me all the time, "Jonathan, what's the most important thing for me to do to get into the school that I want to attend?"

My answer to this question is typically surprising to these kids! It's simple. Separate yourself from everyone else by being likable. And this principle goes beyond just getting into the school you want. The bulleted points that I listed above are all important rules to live by that I know from experience make someone more approachable, coachable, and likeable. I'll say it again (and again and again): much of what makes someone successful is not what they know, but who they know. It's impossible to know people well if you can't develop proper relationships by grasping the concepts I listed above.

I have spoken with a lot of collegiate coaches, and the number one thing they tell me is that athletes can really stand out from the rest by having an engaging and positive personality. I've heard numerous stories from coaches around the country about how awkward some of their conversations are with athletes they are recruiting. Sure, it can be intimidating to have a quick chat with a big university coach, but it's important to remember that they are looking for someone to give potential six-figure scholarships to, and they have to be able to get to know you.

Muster up the courage, step out of the box, be bold, and have an engaging conversation with the coach. Master the skills required to be personable so that not only your future coaches, but also your future team members will see that the light is just a little brighter in your life. You're someone they'll want to be around!

For some reason, young people today are losing their ability to communicate with others effectively. Truthfully, I think it's because technology has caused us all to have our heads down on our phones all day. Regardless, people are forgetting how to really engage with each other.

Coaches want more than talented athletes who can survive the rigors of collegiate courses and difficult training. They are also looking for personable, engaging individuals who will step into leadership roles for their teams. They are looking for someone who knows how to communicate well, puts in work not only for themselves but also for the people around them, and someone who can become an integral part of a tight-knit family. Successful teams become a kind of family, and in order for that to happen, they must be made up of people who know how to develop trusting relationships with one another.

Obviously, people are born with both introverted personalities, extroverted personalities, or some combination of the two, so this may look different for everyone! So when it comes to being a student-athlete, I'm not denying that your talent and grades are important. But if you really want to make yourself stand out, learn to talk to people and develop great relationships. As you move on to the next stages of your life, these skills will come in handy as you understand the value of separating yourself from the competition around you.

Chapter 5

HAVE FUN LATER

Most of us have probably seen, at least once, a movie that revolves around some type of big raging and crazy party. Maybe you've seen *Superbad*, *Van Wilder*, or *Old School*, just to name a few that come to mind. In all of the iconic scenes, people are dancing, singing, drinking beer by the pints and even smoking marijuana.

These scenes look like the most fun any human being could ever imagine, and it can be difficult not to covet this kind of experience in high school and college. I don't really know how to put this in any other way, so I'll just give you my occasionally extremely unpopular advice:

Don't party.

You have big time, elite goals to accomplish!

I had the benefit of not being a super popular kid growing up. Sure, I was known by everyone in school as the gymnastics kid with big biceps, but honestly, I wasn't regularly invited to the big-time parties. I was too busy and too focused on training four to six hours every day. When some of my peers were out being crazy at night, I was finishing my workout at 9 pm and staring at the business end of a lot of homework and a need for rest.

In college, things changed a bit. I was free from any rules at home. I was a "grown up!" I didn't have a bedtime, nobody told me what to eat, drink, when to do my homework, or when I had to be home. Beginning on my first day on campus, I was asked to come out and have a good time with friends and teammates. I hadn't ever been exposed to crazy nights out, and I was tempted in every way to break from my strict schedule.

Fortunately, I stuck to my guns the best that I could. I was the kid in college who didn't drink much. I was the designated driver, and I know I was probably known as the lame guy. I don't say all of this to try to claim that I am "holier than thou," because I made my fair share of poor decisions. But when I was serious about training, what I put into my body mattered.

When I was a senior in high school and just a few weeks away from leaving for college, I had a pretty impactful conversation with a well-known coach. At one point, this particular coach was one of the best gymnasts in the country. He was typically a pretty relaxed guy and a lot of fun to work with, but one afternoon he approached me and I knew immediately that he had something serious to talk about. We sat down to chat for a minute, he looked me in the eye and said, "Jon, don't do what I did. I had a chance to be one of the best in the world, make an Olympic team, and accomplish what I wanted from the sport, but I blew it in college."

He went on to explain to me that in hindsight, he knows that the wild nights of "fun" harmed his training and made him more injury prone. He now believes that because of his poor choices at a crucial time in his career, he never fully reached the pinnacle of the sport.

At this point in my life, I hadn't really even considered the peer pressure and desire I would experience so I didn't fully understand the conversation. I quickly figured it out when I got to school!

During high school and college, I witnessed the repercussions of partying too hard and I knew I didn't want those problems. I didn't have time to spend a few days recovering from a hangover. I didn't want the extra calories and fat from junk food, when I knew that my most important goal was to represent my country at the Olympic games.

I was always aware of the peer pressure and my own desire to have a good time with friends, but the expectation I had for myself to become an Olympian outweighed it all. I can say with 100% certainty that every sacrifice I made to hold off on the fun was worth it. Standing on the awards podium at the Olympics, watching my flag rise, and knowing I was one of the greatest gymnasts in the world was worth every sacrifice I ever made.

I've spoken to a few athletes before who say that if they could go back in time and do everything again, one of the aspects of their life that they would have eased up on was the amount that they partied. You see, it's not necessarily that going to a party is a bad idea, but it's really the alcohol consumption that comes with it that can destroy an athlete. It may not rough you up in the beginning, but give it a minute. It's going to take a toll.

I had to not only sacrifice the crazy experiences and "fun" that I knew a lot of people were having, but I also had to distance myself from people whose choices and actions weren't conducive to the lifestyle I knew I needed to sustain. All of the sacrifices were worth it, though, because I accomplished my goals. I became an Olympian.

Hold off on the parties. Sacrifice the fun now for the glory later. Don't give in to the peer pressure from people who will never understand how badly you want what it is you want. Save that kind of fun for later and you'll thank yourself for it.

Chapter 6

DON'T FORGET THE BASICS

I had a conversation once with a magician who told me that the majority of people who find out how a trick is done are typically incredibly disappointed with just how simple it is. Magic is all about creating the illusion of something impossible - grand, mysterious, mind-blowing. However, what makes a magician great isn't being able to pull off the trick as a whole, but, rather, being able to master simple and minute details that other magicians aren't willing to spend the time mastering. In the end, a trick can be mesmerizing, but the truth is that the magician is just better than others at basic skills to make an intricate trick appear simple to execute.

People are always shocked when I tell them that my sport was no different than a magician mastering basics like sleight of hand, because I had to master basics myself. Every single day, regardless of the level, the first thing that I did in my training sessions was spend 30-45 minutes on foundational elements of gymnastics. They included swinging on the parallel bars, circling the pommel horse, even cartwheels and forward rolls on the floor exercise.

These were the same skills that a coach would work on with a five-year-old, and here I was in my late 20s and early 30s, at the end of my career, still focusing on how to make these simple things just a little better. Not a single day went by in my gymnastics career that I didn't take serious time and focus to develop my basic elements.

I knew that mastery of the swing on parallel bars could lead to more power and higher dismounts, a faster cartwheel led into a faster double backflip on floor, and a more elevated circle on the pommel horse led to a more efficient and less exhausting routine. In the end people watched me and other Olympians and probably just saw gymnasts doing high flying and exciting gymnastics. In our minds, though, we were just putting the full understanding of basic elements to work.

Take time every single day to master the basic, and perhaps simple, pieces of your craft. You don't have to devote a lot of time or even a ton of effort, but consistency is the key. Do them every day so that, even without too much thought, the skills develop all by themselves. A young child who does forward rolls doesn't need coaching to make a forward roll better. If they just keep doing them every day, they will improve by their own innate ability to problem-solve with their minds and bodies to make things better.

The world loves to see the final product; the multi-million-dollar business, the professional athlete, the surgeon, the lawyer, or the famous actor/actress. What is demonstrated by the experts in every field is the tip of the iceberg of the skills that they actually have. Nobody becomes great at anything without first mastering the basics.

Whether you are five or 50, continue to focus on the minutiae and basics of what it takes to be great. It's easy (and tempting) to slip into thinking that it isn't necessary to work on foundational skills anymore. But I promise you - when the foundation cracks, everything else will come crashing down with it. These things that are so easy to do, are also easy not to do. Just choose to get them done.

Chapter 7

USE THE RIGHT FUEL

As a young kid, I could eat anything I wanted. I still felt good and never gained a single pound. I was invincible and didn't believe that the food I put in my body made a difference.

Cereal, pizza, burgers, soda, candy, fast food - it didn't matter. I ate it all and I ate it often. I remember going to the lunch lines in school and having the option of healthy food or junk food. I didn't choose the responsible, healthy options a single time!

I look back to those times and I am disgusted by my choices and by my lack of knowledge regarding diet and nutrition. Around the age of 24 or 25, I felt a significant shift in my body. That's right, I said 24 or 25. That means that at my first Olympic Games, at the age of 22, I was eating junk. Please don't be like me! My teammates at the 2008 Olympics thought I was crazy as I piled the food high and topped it off with a nice big coke. They were right!

My diet eventually caught up to me, and my performance struggled significantly. I was eating the same old junk food but blaming my athletic issues on other things. I was convinced I wasn't training hard enough, or I was maybe just having an off season. It wasn't until I finally let go of my pride that I realized I was gaining weight and feeling weak because of my poor diet.

When I was struggling to keep my body running the way it always had, someone suggested that I seek out a certified nutritionist. Let's just say that was a tough meeting. I was told I needed to completely overhaul my diet. The changes were really difficult to make, and I hated every moment of it. Slowly, but surely:

- Cereal became egg whites, toast, and fruit.
- Pizza rolls and taquitos became grilled chicken and veggies.
- Coke became water.

I'm almost embarrassed to talk about what I used to put in my body, but I know I'm not alone in taking the easy way out of proper nutrition.

At the age of 25, after making drastic changes in my diet, I was the strongest, fastest, and most lean I had ever been. The feeling of being light and powerful made my gymnastics feel easier than ever before. When I think back on my first Olympics at 22, I can't help but imagine what kind of machine I would have been at a younger age by simply eating differently. That's the point I want to drive home!

So maybe you're a young athlete. Maybe you're reading this thinking, "I know I don't have a great diet now, but look at Jon! He made the Olympics with an awful diet. I'll be fine for a few more years and then I'll change my ways."

If that's you, get that thought out of your mind, NOW! Yes, I did some great stuff with junk for fuel in my body, but one of my few regrets is not taking advantage of my body when it was in its prime. I wish that I had taken my nutrition seriously when I was younger. Who knows what more I could have accomplished! Sure, it's possible that I wouldn't have done anything better. But still, I wish I could look back and know that I gave myself that little edge.

With the knowledge that we now have in the world of proper diet and nutrition, there really is no excuse for not understanding performance- based nutrition. Knowledge is just a quick Google search away.

Being an elite athlete is a one-time shot. We only get one body, and we need to fuel it properly. Most people have probably heard the analogy that our bodies are like a Top Fuel drag car—or maybe a better analogy is to compare ourselves to a Lamborghini or Ferrari. We would never, in a million years, put low-grade fuel into a high-performance vehicle like one of those. So why would we put poor fuel into our bodies?

If you want to be great, make the sacrifice to eat right. Do some studying and find what makes your body function at its highest level. I messed this part up for the first three-quarters of my career. You don't have to!

Chapter 8

GO TO BED!

This chapter will be a quick one because the idea is plain and simple.

Go to sleep.

As a college student, I experienced some of the most exhausting days of my life. I had 6:00 am training sessions, followed by class, followed by another training in the afternoon, then I returned to evening classes, went home, ate and studied, and woke up the next morning to do it all again. No matter what, I forced myself to go to sleep and get a minimum of eight hours. I tell people about my college schedule all the time, and I always have someone ask me, "Well, what if you have a project due, or an exam the next day and you have to pull an all-nighter?"

My answer is, "Stop procrastinating until the last minute to study or get your work done!"

I had teammates in school who would stay up until 2 am and wake up at 5:30 am consistently. They looked like zombies. There is no doubt in my mind that their performance abilities were hurt by their lack of sleep.

I will admit, I was pretty good about rest and recovery, which in hindsight probably balanced out some of my terrible diet. Sleep habits for an elite athlete are just as important as any other aspect of training, especially as you get older and become engulfed with intense studies and stress from school and work.

Our bodies heal and recover at night while we sleep better than any other time. I have even read studies that show the best way to recover after a hard practice is to immediately eat and take a 30-minute to one-hour nap after a training session.

- Put the video games away (I have to remind myself to do that from time to time) …
- Stop watching late-night movies…
- Shut Netflix down…
- Get your studying done at an appropriate time…

... and go to sleep! If you want to take your training to the next level, some of these fun nighttime activities have to be held to a minimum or sometimes sacrificed altogether. Believe me, it's worth it.

Chapter 9

WHO DO YOU WANT TO BE?

I have always been a big dreamer. When I watched the Olympics for the first time in 1996, I saw people win gold medals, and I imagined myself one day doing the same. When I watched the USA National Championships and saw Blaine Wilson win the national title, I could feel my body flying through the air like his, and experiencing the joy of being the champion. When I watched the NCAA National Championships and saw teams win their National Championship rings, I felt the same intensity of those college teams running through my veins.

I was lucky to have heroes that I looked up to from the time I was a kid. My heroes were superstars in the world of gymnastics like Bart Conner, Blaine Wilson, John Roethlisberger, Alexei Nemov, and Li Xiaopeng.

Bart Conner was an iconic Olympian in the '80s because he led Team USA to the first-ever gymnastics Gold medal at the Olympics. Bart always appeared to compete with so much joy; smiling, waving to the crowd, and rallying his team.

Blaine Wilson was the aggressive competitor who reigned supreme as the four-time National Champion. Blaine was the fiercest competitor I have ever seen in my sport. I'll never forget watching the US Nationals on TV as a young kid, and seeing Blaine burst into a rage because he didn't do a routine the way he wanted. He was a lion on the competitive stage, and he made it clear that he wasn't okay with losing.

John Roethlisberger was the ultimate leader in the '90s. He was a multiple-time National Champion and three-time Olympian. He was greater than Captain America in my eyes. I always felt his passion and commitment to the USA more than anyone else, and I, too, wanted to lead my team the way he did for so many years.

There were even international competitors who had a big impact on my career, like Alexei Nemov, the Russian icon who won the Olympic All-Around title at the

2000 Olympics. He changed the sport with his perfect performances and outgoing personality.

Finally, there was my favorite gymnast of all time, Li Xiaopeng from China. There hasn't ever been another gymnast who did more extreme gymnastics. He was radical, and it was awesome! Li Xiaopeng made me realize that nothing was impossible. Throughout the years, people in the gymnastics world continue to say that we have reached the peak of the sport. They will say that the sport can't get harder, there is no way someone can do a more difficult skills, it's impossible to advance further. Xiaopeng used to do things that put those ideas to shame, and he did it with a smile on his face. One of my greatest memories in the sport was having the opportunity to compete against Xiaopeng at the 2008 Olympics. It's one thing to meet an idol who inspires us. It's a whole different experience to get to compete against them after admiring them for so many years.

What is important here is that I had idols who I aspired to imitate and a vision of success that I wanted to experience. All the men that I've mentioned have had a major impact on who I finally became as an athlete. I'd like to think that I have a small piece of every one of their styles that I have painted into my own masterpiece.

Here's a question I get all the time; "Jon, when you're struggling or feeling burned out, what keeps you motivated to push through?"

My answer is, "I have an image in my head of who I want to be and what I want to accomplish, and if that image hasn't become a reality, I try to close my eyes and remind myself of the vision daily."

It's easy to have a goal, but it's a little more challenging to find a way to get there. One of the most important things you can do is to have a model or a blueprint of the steps you need to take. Don't reinvent the wheel of success, ask someone what to do or research what someone else did to accomplish what you want.

It's important that you know what the success you are aiming for looks like, so that when motivation is low and you're feeling burned out, you can close your eyes, remember what it looked like when you first saw someone accomplish what you want, and remind yourself of why you started this journey to begin with.

I never wanted to be any of the people who I looked up to; I wanted to be better. However, I did want to use the path that they had already paved in front of me to find my way.

One of the most valuable pieces of advice I received was to seek out advice from a mentor. Once I realized the value of having someone successful teach me what they knew, I wanted more. I strongly encourage you to go out and find a mentor! If you're lucky enough to reach the top level of your sport, you may have the privilege, like I did, to someday be mentored by one of your heroes.

I know this sounds ridiculous, but when I retired from gymnastics, I got into utility sales. Truth is, I had a time in my life when I was struggling to transition from gymnastics into a steady career. I needed to make some extra money, so I thought, "What the heck, I'll try something completely out of my comfort zone."

When I got involved in the company, one of my business partners was an extremely successful millionaire who took me under his wing. He said to me when I got started, "Jon, have you ever had a mentor before?"

I thought about it for a second, and finally said, "No."

I had a lot of people I looked up to, but I had never sought out someone who I could consistently count on to help me or give me good advice. Having him as a mentor really helped me wrap my mind around how to properly transition from gymnastics, understand business, network with new people, and use my old experiences and expertise to grow into something new.

Don't be afraid to seek out a mentor. Go find someone who has accomplished what you want and ask them questions. If you can't get in touch with them, study their every move on social media and websites. Most successful people document their sports or business and are easy to follow. Use your resources to study. In today's age, there is every single resource imaginable at the touch of a button on a computer or phone. There is no excuse to not become knowledgeable and to find someone who knows the answers. There isn't a person on this planet who has the "secret" to success. There are no secrets anymore, you just have to be willing to go seek out the answers to your questions.

I eventually surrounded myself with all types of successful people. I have heard on multiple occasions that you are the average of your five closest friends, mentally, physically, spiritually, emotionally, and financially. I wholeheartedly believe it!

If there is one thing I know for sure, it's that people love to give their opinion. Make sure you find people with opinions that count. Take what they say seriously and let them hold you accountable to your goals and promises.

Success has already been accomplished in every sport, job, and business, so you don't need to discover a new way to succeed. See it, want it, remember it, and let someone who has done it show you how to do it.

Chapter 10

SURROUND YOURSELF
WITH GREATNESS

Through most phases of my career I was fortunate enough to have an exceptional team around me. I have no doubt that without that team, I wouldn't have become the athlete that I finally became. No, we didn't always get along, but we were a group of men on the same mission. We were competitive and driven towards the next big step, and in moments of failure or struggle we had each other's backs.

I remember days when I was angry because of a particular skill or routine that I couldn't learn, simply because a member of my team learned it faster. The feeling drove me to work harder. I hated not being caught up with the other athletes. There were days when I thought I was too tired to continue my strength training, but someone else would be plowing through it with no problem. It kept me from quitting. I needed my solid team so that we could all rise together. Nobody was a weak link. We all wanted to be winners.

When I competed for the University of Oklahoma, I started to really grasp how important it is to be surrounded by like-minded people. My college coach was unshakably stern about who would represent our team on the competitive floor. Our team had coach's way, and then there was the highway. Coach wouldn't think twice to kick the best guy off the team if he didn't buy into the system.

I'll never forget the day that I was punished for being late to practice. It only happened once, and it was my senior year. We had a rule on the team that if you were late, you had to do extra conditioning. I had never been late to a work out before, but a week before the conference championships, I showed up late to an afternoon workout. I can't remember why I was late, but I broke the rule of not only being late, but also to make matters worse, I didn't call coach to let him know ahead of time. I walked into the gym, and he told me that before training started, I had to do 100 dips on parallel bars, and they were on top of our regular conditioning circuit.

I looked at him and I said, "Coach, come on! This is the first time I have ever been late in four years of being at this school. You have to let this slide."

He responded back to me, "No, I don't. Go do your dips."

Everyone could see that I was visibly frustrated, but I walked over to the bars and did my dips.

I look back now and I see that my coach was only doing what was right for the team as a whole. We were a phenomenal group of athletes, but he couldn't let anyone slide, not even a senior who at the time was ranked fourth in the world.

Coach taught me how important it is to know that you are only as strong as the weakest link. I feel fortunate to have been on a team with a coach who showed us that if we took care of each other first, respected the system, and worked our butts off, the national championship title would follow.

Success first begins with a dream or a goal, and the motivation to pursue it. Next, you need the vision and game plan to make it happen. Finally, you need massive, radical action. Within those steps, there is something important that must not be missed—the right team around you.

I know that I have already touched on this, but I really want to hammer it in: you won't get far without the right people to push you along the way.

If you spend time with winners, you will most likely become a winner.

If you spend your time with millionaires, you will pick up tools to help you become financially successful.

If you spend your time with those who are content with doing the bare minimum, you'll find yourself in the same boat.

Mentally, physically, emotionally, spiritually, and financially, you are the product of your associations. Whether you are an aspiring athlete, professional athlete, novice entrepreneur or a billionaire, everyone needs people around them who bring them up and hold them accountable to their goals and their values.

I believe in being straightforward and blunt, so here goes...

Too many times I see people who claim they want to live a big life, but they hang out with losers. Big. Giant. Losers. I don't totally understand it, but there are people in this world who only want to drag you down. Those people don't have the ambition to wake up swinging every morning, and they don't want to see the people that do make anything of themselves.

Get away!

Run away as fast as you can from those who choose mediocrity. Find the people in this world who will give an arm and a leg to see you succeed. Trust me – they're out there! They are extremely rare, but they exist. You just have to diligently seek them out.

The team of people you surround yourself with is essential to your success. You will rise and fall with the people you spend your time with. You know what? We will all fall at some point. Make sure you've surrounded yourself with people who want to see you get back up as badly as you do.

Chapter 11

TEAM FIRST

If I had to identify the most important, life-altering lesson from my time as a gymnast, it would be that the most powerful way to succeed is to view other people's success as more important than your own.

When I was a young kid, I had a big dream of being an Olympian. I dreamed about someday standing on the Olympic podium in front of 50,000 people, watching the American flag rise, and having gold medal after gold medal placed around my neck. I wanted to be an Olympic hero who people shouted about from the rooftops.

That dream drove me every day in the gym while I trained. When I would compete, I used to think about how much closer I was getting to that moment. Every time I would win a medal, ribbon, or trophy, I would think about how I could be better and win more.

Did I need to do more routines?

Did I need to train longer hours?

How could I make the person who was better than me look worse?

My competitive drive pushed me to want to be the best, and I never really cared about anyone else but myself—until I got to college.

When I arrived at the University of Oklahoma in the summer of 2004, I instantly had a large group of teammates who had also been training their entire lives to be some of the best gymnasts in the country. Not long after starting school, I found myself having slightly different goals than the rest of the group. The whole team was always talking about winning the National Championship. The guys would get so excited when they talked about beating other teams like Stanford, Ohio State, Michigan, Illinois, and Penn State; some of the best teams around when I was competing. I honestly didn't really care about beating those teams. I just wanted to win four individual all-around titles and make the Olympic team when I was finished with my education.

I look back and laugh, because I was quickly forced to change my way of thinking. I was the snotty little freshman gymnast who thought he was a "rockstar" when I got to school. Fortunately for me, the team had seven seniors who wanted to make the most of their last year of competition. Those guys were not going to let some punk—who cared only about himself—ruin their last year of gymnastics. From a little light razzing to some serious sit-down talks, those seven seniors encouraged me to see the bigger picture. I not only looked up to them, but I loved them like family. My mindset shifted quickly after spending so much time with my new teammates, and I eventually found myself wanting to see them win more than I wanted it for myself.

There was a culture on our team at OU that made me realize that there was more satisfaction in winning together. My freshman year was full of ups and downs as I learned what it meant to be a team player, but in the end, we won the national title. For the first time I got a taste of what it felt like to stand on top of an award podium with the men I had gone to battle with all year. That rush of adrenaline and intense joy was something I wanted to create more of, and there was no going back to my selfish ways.

In my four years of competition in college, I went on to win six individual NCAA titles. I received eighteen All-American honors and my team won three out of four national championships. My junior year we lost the NCAA National Championship to Penn State - I would trade every single individual title that I own to have won the team competition my junior year instead of placing second, and I can say that without hesitation.

The late Zig Ziglar once said, "You can have everything you want in life, if you will just help other people get what they want."

His statement is one of the truest statements in history. In the latter part of my athletic career, I was always able to rise to a higher level when I knew my team needed me. There is something powerful about wanting to see the people I cared about succeed more than I wanted it for myself.

So when I did a routine in competition, I was no longer only focused exclusively on me. Instead, I was focused on how my performance would affect my team, and that focus gave me super strength! When I was in front of a billion people at the Olympics, I wasn't nervous because I wanted to win. I was nervous because I couldn't stand the idea of not coming through for the other five men who had poured their blood, sweat, and tears into also becoming Olympic champions.

I'm eternally grateful to my college team for showing me that when I put my team before myself to help everyone win, I was able to win, too.

To my Oklahoma Sooner brothers and coaches, thank you.

Chapter 12

GO DOWN SWINGING

One of the most rewarding competitions of my entire career was in 2009 at the World Championships. As with many other impactful events in my life, I didn't realize how rewarding the experience was until well after it was over.

I was on the World Championship team that competed in London. I was coming off the most successful year I had ever had. I had earned two Olympic medals, and I was the current USA National All-Around Champion. People had high hopes for me as an All-Arounder at Worlds that year.

I began the competition and immediately started feeling a little off. I had the shakes, and to this day, I'm not totally sure why. It was maybe a combination of nerves and pressure that I was putting on myself to live up to expectations. I had a hard time performing during the warm-up session, but I had felt bad before, so I told myself to shake it off and get the job done.

On my first event (floor), I fell on my very first skill. My legs were shaking, and I knew there was something wrong. I fought through and finished the routine thinking to myself that all wasn't lost yet. Then I went to pommel horse and fell two more times.

At this point during the World Championships, there was no coming back from three falls. I was dead in the water, but I still had four more routines to complete. It would have looked pretty bad if I just walked out.

I told my coach that I had never felt this off before, and he was sympathetic, given the circumstances. He asked me what I wanted to do, and I said, "I'm finishing the meet."

My rings routine and my vault were subpar, and I was in last place going into the last two events. I'm sure the other athletes were wondering why I was still even in the arena, but I gave it my all on the parallel bars and high bar, and somehow put up the biggest scores of the night on those two events. I still finished nearly last place, and I was beyond embarrassed and upset, but it wasn't until later that I realized that I had done something special.

In the biggest competition in gymnastics—with the exception of the Olympics—I showed tenacity. I showed my heart for my sport, and I never gave up, even when I should have. I continued to be as aggressive as my body would allow me to be with every routine I performed. Many athletes and coaches came up to me and told me that it was great to see me rise up at the end of the competition, although there was basically nothing to gain from it. Lord knows, it would have been a heck of a lot easier to throw in the towel.

Let's just get this out of the way. You're going to lose. No ifs, ands or buts about it. You will make mistakes. You may fall at a competition, be the player who blows it for the rest of the team or make a mental mistake that makes everyone question whether you can ever recover.

Making mistakes is a big part of life! The question is how you handle the defeat in the moment, and how you handle defeat after it's over. Do you leave the moment overwhelmed and hold back when you know problems are snowballing, or do you choose to fight to the bitter end?

Always fight.

If there is one thing I can guarantee to every athlete, it's that you'll recover faster after a hard-fought battle even if it ends in a loss. The worst thing that you can do is to give up when you face certain defeat.

We all want to be winners, but it just isn't going to happen every time. My hope is that nobody begins training for their sport simply because they want to win stuff. I hope you started your sport or career because of a love for it. When you love your sport, whether you win first or place last, you grind it out and fight until the very end of the game, match, or competition. If you're going to fall or fail, it's a heck of a lot better to go down swinging than it is to be a quitter.

Every single moment matters, win or lose. In the losses, there will be a lesson to soak in even if your clothing is also soaking in your tears. Wipe them away and move forward. Stay in attack mode and be aggressive! You will make yourself not only a better athlete, but a stronger human being for never giving up.

Trust me, I know what it will do for you to grit it out when you want to quit.

In 2010, at the same competition I bombed the year before, I became the fourth American male gymnast to ever stand on the awards podium as an All-Around World Medalist.

Never quit.

Chapter 13

MAKE SOMETHING OUT OF NOTHING

Throughout my gymnastics career, one of the most challenging aspects of performing well was that it depended on how good my hands felt. All but two of men's gymnastics events require rigorous use of the hands, and if our hands were battered, bruised, and ripped, it made for a miserable experience.

From the time I was a kid, my coach was pretty hard on me when it came to being tired with torn up hands. Truth is, as I became more advanced, there were more days when I felt bad than good ones; it was just part of being at the elite level. Day after day, I had to train myself to deal with pain and discomfort and learn that it wasn't an excuse.

I didn't totally understand the value of pushing through in this manner until 2010, when I competed at the World Championships in Rotterdam, Netherlands. I was the kind of athlete who got super psyched up and adrenaline-pumped for any competition. The World Championships and the Olympics were the ultimate events for me, so I always told myself that there was no way I would ever compete at a big event and not feel good. Unfortunately, in 2010, I faced a battle similar to Michael Jordan's, which I'll explain a little later in the chapter.

I qualified into the All-Around final, which included the top 25 gymnasts from around the world. As the current American National Champion, I was also one of the best worldwide. Only three American male gymnasts before me had ever won an All-Around medal at a World Championships, and I knew it was possible for me to be the fourth.

A few weeks before the competition, I was training on the parallel bars when I got a blister on my hand (also known as a "rip" in gymnastics) that was the size of a silver dollar. It was extremely deep, and it was tough to get it to stop bleeding. I hadn't ever had a rip that big before, and there weren't many gymnasts or coaches had ever seen anything like it, either.

I struggled to train leading up to the competition, so I had to get creative with my training to stay in shape. Leading up to the meet, my hand would heal a little, then tear, heal a little again, and then tear again. There just wasn't enough time for it to recover.

Despite the pain I was enduring throughout my routines, I was somehow able to have one of the greatest competitions in my career during the finals. Routine after routine, I felt my hand rip open just a little more, bleed a little more, and give me more discomfort. Specifically, on my parallel bar routine, which requires the most extreme use of our hands, I felt my blood pool under my hand, which made me nearly slip. I squeezed with everything I had, did one of my best routines ever, and at the end of the competition I won the bronze medal and made history for Team USA.

There is absolutely no doubt in my mind that without the years and years of developing the right mindset, I wouldn't have been able to accomplish what I did.

We all have bad days. Every single person on the planet has woken up in the morning, hit the snooze button ten times, felt irritable, and had zero desire to get anything done. It's completely normal.

These are some of the most important days for an athlete or entrepreneur. It's the bad days, when we have nothing left, our bodies hurt, and we don't want to train, that can sometimes bring about our most valuable training moments. There will be days when you are tired, sore, and mentally unfocused. Your job during those moments is to reach down into your soul and make something happen.

No matter how good or bad you feel, every single day counts. Every day brings a new opportunity to inch a little bit closer to your goals, and there is always a way to keep pushing regardless of how you feel. Even if you can't accomplish much on that day, find a way to keep moving. You never know how you're going to feel when something important is on the line.

A perfect example is Michael Jordan in 1997 in the NBA finals. Jordan will always be remembered for one of the most phenomenal performances in all of basketball history, when he summoned something special inside of himself. During that game, he scored 38 points and clinched a game-winning three-pointer—with the flu. His teammate, Scottie Pippen, can be seen in iconic photos carrying his exhausted teammate after the win.

There is no doubt that Jordan was an all-around special player, but even the greatest have to learn how to handle the worst of days. The mental capacity to accomplish something like Jordan did isn't possible without treating every day as important and developing a strong mindset.

The ability to make something happen out of nothing is a learned skill of an elite athlete; nobody is born with it. It takes time and consistency to master the mindset of making every day count. While it's easy to feel amazing, work hard, and succeed, it's incredibly difficult to feel horrible and continue to put in an identical effort with the same results. Truth be told, the days in which we feel like pure garbage, yet still perform at full capacity, are the ones which separate the good people from the great ones.

Chapter 14

1%

Anyone who is a fan of gymnastics knows that a perfect score is a 10.0. There is the hole-in-one, the full-court swish, the 80-yard Hail Mary, and the perfect 10.0. None are as rare as the 10.0 in elite gymnastics. Over the entirety of my gymnastics career, I only witnessed two people ever accomplish the elusive score. One of those people was me. I only did it once. I was eleven years old, performing a simple vault. I ran down an 82-foot vault runway, hit a bouncy spring board, and flew over the apparatus. I performed the easiest vault done in the sport, but I guess I did it perfectly.

When I saw that 10.0 on the scoreboard, I was pretty pumped!

After that moment, I never saw the judges' raise that score for one of my routines again. I got plenty of 9.8s and 9.9s, but my days of the 10.0 were over.

There was one other day in my life that I considered myself to be perfect, though, and it began with a dream.

I used to dream every night of this scenario: I imagined myself at the Olympic games, wearing red, white, and blue. I would be the last gymnast up on the high bar, and I would have to nail it for Team USA to win.

That vision was so strong that I trained my entire life to make the moment a reality. I am happy to say that I got close.

When I made the Olympic team in 2008, I was beyond ecstatic. I traveled across the world to Beijing, China to finally stand as an Olympian. I had never had what I liked to call, "a perfect day." Male gymnasts have six events, and I always thought it would be amazing to make zero mistakes in a competition, and stick all of my dismounts. Sticking a dismount in gymnastics means that when the athlete leaves the apparatus and lands on the ground, they plant their feet into the mats and don't move. It's like throwing a dart into a dart board, but much more difficult.

I had never had a major competition in which I was even half-perfect, but somehow, in front of 40,000 people watching live and a billion more watching from their television screens, I nailed every single routine and stuck every single dismount.

In other words, I had my perfect day.

I am a perfectionist to the core. I want everything to be done right with the most extreme attention to detail. I have a feeling most aspiring elite and professional athletes can relate.

What is the cost of being a perfectionist, though? The answer is frustration. So as a perfectionist, the only day in my gymnastics career that was completely satisfying and not at all frustrating, was that day in 2008!

If you're like me, when something doesn't go exactly the way you plan it, it's easy to blow your top. My greatest struggle was controlling my frustration. I wasn't the most talented kid in the gym, and I had some lofty goals. When I found myself behind everyone else, I wasn't okay.

In fact, I was the kid who cried during practice, threw temper tantrums, and yelled, "I QUIT!" more times than

I care to remember during training. Inevitably, though, I always came back.

As I advanced as an athlete, of course, I matured to a point where the crying stopped. The anger, however, seemed to grow more intense! I just wanted to be the best so badly that I couldn't handle it, and my coaches could see that. My anger and frustration came from my desire to improve and perform better, but the inability to control those emotions was also slowing me down.

One of the best pieces of advice I continually received from my coach was, "Jonathan, remember that you're only going to be perfect 1% of the time."

In the beginning, when I heard him say that, I let it go in one ear and out the other, and I didn't let myself truly comprehend what he meant. Eventually, though, I realized that what my coach was telling me translated to, "Jonathan, it's okay that you aren't perfect. Calm down and let's focus on pursuing the 1% moment. It doesn't happen every day, but let's try to enjoy the process."

Getting angry over your performance is natural to some extent. However, it's important to learn to master not only the physical and mental side of our sports, but also the emotional.

You will lose. You will have hard days, and you will want to quit. I guarantee it! But if you can master your emotions, you'll be able to regain your elite mindset much faster.

It took me many years to master my emotions, and I still struggle with it. My instincts still tell me to give everything I have to my pursuit and if I'm not instantly the best, I can get angry. I have to remind myself to stay calm, focus on the goal, and focus on a day-to-day process and grind that is necessary to get there.

I hated many moments of training because I couldn't get things done the way I wanted. I always wanted to be the best, but it felt like it would never happen. I had to wait for eighteen years before I finally saw that my coach was right about how often I would be perfect. At the Olympic games in 2008, I had my 1% moment. I won two medals for my country. I was the best I had ever been and, finally, close to "perfect."

So, my encouragement for you is to stay patient and maintain proper perspective. Most of your days will fall into the 99%. Wait on that 1% moment because it is completely worth it!

Chapter 15

DO ONE MORE

One of my weaknesses as a gymnast was the ability to "stick" a landing. On every apparatus, gymnasts have to do a dismount and land on their feet without moving them afterward. Moving your feet after they hit the ground incurs a penalty. The dismount can be anything from a simple backflip to multiple twists and flips. Regardless of what my dismount was, though, I always struggled to plant my feet into the ground and not move them.

Because sticking my dismount was such a weakness for me, I wouldn't let myself leave the event or be finished with my routine until I stuck a dismount. I had days when I would be on an event for an extra twenty to thirty minutes doing everything in my power to stick my dismount, but I just couldn't time it appropriately.

On many occasions my coaches and teammates would see that I was visibly frustrated and potentially making myself worse, and they would urge me to just move on and work on it tomorrow. I always looked at them and said, "Nah, I just gotta do one more." Eventually, I would stick my dismount and move on to the next event.

To this day, with the level of frustration I had from moments like this, I'm still not totally sure whether doing extremely taxing dismounts onto hard-landing mats helped me or hurt me. I was kicked out of the gym on multiple occasions, and my coaches would yell at me to go to the next event when I hadn't finished doing what I wanted to do (that always made me so mad). The only evidence that I have to back up my style of training is the fact that under pressure, at the biggest moments of my career, I stuck my dismounts. I made mistakes and fell every day in training, but at the NCAA championships, I stuck it; at the national championships, I stuck it; at the World Championships, I stuck it; and at the Olympic games—yep, you got it; I stuck everything.

Don't ever leave a training session with unfinished business.

Try out my simple advice, and "Do one more."

Catch one more pass, hit one more ball, run one more lap, practice one more drill. Take one more practice test to prepare for school. Make one more phone call for your business.

We have all witnessed people who excel at doing the bare minimum. I can almost promise you that they will never rise above mediocrity. There is a giant difference between doing 100% of the work and going beyond 100%. Over the years, I have witnessed some of the most talented athletes in the world fail to accomplish any big goals because they chose to do exactly what they were told, no more and no less.

Want to be great? Go above and beyond what you're being told to do. Take a workout plan and double it. Work so hard that your coach has to tell you to stop and your teammates wonder what is wrong with you.

If you want to be great, you have to do more than your competition. Some people say you have to train hard; some people say you have to train smart. I say you can do both at the same time. There is no substitute for repetition and building the mental endurance to keep pushing.

Like I said, I have seen some of the most phenomenally talented people accomplish absolutely nothing by the end of their career because they do the bare minimum.

Don't be that person.

Chapter 16

TAKE THE SHOT

It's funny to me how even at the peak of our careers, people will still doubt us. Moments of great opportunity with high risk can present themselves, and we still hear talk about how we aren't good enough for the moment.

I shouldn't have won a silver medal at the Olympics— at least that's what a lot people that know all the details say. I wasn't supposed to be one of the best in the world, but I was.

Once again, let me take you back to the beginning of my career.

When I was 13 years old, I started to get into the groove of gymnastics. It had taken me awhile to catch my stride, but I was getting stronger and learning rapidly. I still had some pretty bad struggles, though.

My nemesis was always the pommel horse. You know, that silly-looking rectangular thing with the handles on top? Yeah, I sucked at the pommel horse my entire career. What a lot of people outside of the sport don't know is that I was also horrendous on the high bar growing up.

If you don't know what the high bar is, that's okay. It's a giant steel bar that stands 10 feet off the ground and gymnasts circle around it using nothing but our hands; sounds smart, right?

In my opinion—and I think most people's opinions—the high bar is the most exciting and high-flying event in the sport. I've always thought that it could easily make its way into the X-games.

Anyway, with as much as I loved highbar, I really struggled at this time in my training. I just couldn't really figure out how to do the widely-accepted skills that most guys my age were learning! There were a bunch of little intricate twists and turns and ways of manipulating our bodies that my body just wasn't accepting.

I was quickly finding myself far behind my teammates and other competitors. That struggle was super frustrating until one eye-opening day in front of the TV.

I can't recall the name of the competition I was watching, but one afternoon I was watching gymnastics on TV, and I saw one of the athletes swinging rapidly around a high bar. Suddenly, he let go of the bar, did a double backflip, and then he grabbed the bar.

Now, I had seen this skill before, but for whatever reason, this time the giant light bulb went off in my brain and I developed a rather wild idea. I started thinking to myself, "I can't really do any of that other stuff on this event, but maybe I can do one of those crazy flips over the bar and catch it."

So, I went back into my gym for my next practice session and told my coach and a few of my teammates about my idea. Coach looked at me and said, "Yeah, that skill is called a Kovacs. It's one of the hardest skills being done in the world. You aren't ready for that."

I remember thinking to myself, "Apparently, I'm not ready for any of this other stuff either, because I can't master any of it!"

I was having such a difficult time learning what were supposed to be the "simple" and "appropriate" skills for my age that I had developed an attitude of, "What's the worst that could happen by trying something new?"

If there was one personality trait that might've helped me more than anything else in gymnastics, it's that I wasn't ever afraid to go big. A lot of young gymnasts are terrified of the high bar because, well, it's a steel high bar 10 feet in the air. That's pretty reasonable! But that wasn't me. I might not have been the best, but I wasn't scared.

Coach told me I wasn't allowed to try the Kovacs, but just to pacify me, he allowed me to work on the special type of set up swinging that is required to get the height and rotation necessary for the skill. It's also known as the tap swing.

I worked on the tap swing for a few months, and I got bored. I wasn't allowed to actually try the skill, but I had it in my mind that I could do it. One day when my coach wasn't paying attention, I got up the nerve to just swing around the bar as fast as I could and let go. Something special happened; I didn't die. In fact, it wasn't that bad, so I kept trying it, over and over again.

I caught my first Kovacs on the second day of ever trying it, and I was the only 13-year-old in the country who could do one. Needless to say, I was pumped, and the gym erupted in cheers and claps every time I caught one.

So now, I was a young kid with a grown-up skill. But now what? It was the only thing I really knew how to do well on the high bar, so I made the decision to roll with it. I found my niche and I was going to maximize it for all that it was worth.

I got the idea that I should stop focusing so much on the stuff that I wasn't good at, and just go all out with the one thing I knew I was meant to do. I decided I was just going to do a crazy high-flying routine with different variations of a Kovacs.

I learned how to do it in the straight and bent-legged positions, with a twist, and with different leg positions while twisting. I started performing a high bar routine that was completely out of the ordinary and unique in the gymnastics world. It was also incredibly risky - not only to complete it successfully, but also risky to my safety. No other gymnasts in the world were flying over the bar, doing double backflips, and catching the bar multiple times in one routine. I was the only lunatic, but I loved it.

At the age of 14, I started competing a routine that had three extremely high-level and risky Kovacs elements. It was exciting and unique compared to other gymnasts, but I was rarely able to complete it successfully. Competition after competition, I would fall off the bar. Fortunately for my eventual elite career, my coach let me keep trying because, well, I wasn't any good at anything else.

I'll never forget the day that one of the top coaches in the country approached me with a serious look on his face and said, "Stop it. Stop doing that routine. You will never be able to perform a routine like that under pressure. If you ever become an elite gymnast, you will never be able to complete that routine at a major international competition like the Olympics."

But I persisted. Over many years of trial and error and approximately one billion falls, I gained the ability to perform the elements under pressure. Before I knew it, I was the highest ranked gymnast in the country on high bar. The routine was a crowd pleaser, judges loved seeing something different, and I loved performing it!

My high-bar routine was going well and steadily improving until the year of the Olympics in 2008. I still can't figure out what happened, but in 2008, the most important year of my competitive life, I went back in time and fell on almost every single high bar routine I competed.

It had been almost ten years since beginning this wild high bar journey, and at the pinnacle season of my career, everything was crashing down (literally). I couldn't catch the bar to save my life, and the people who told me it was impossible in the beginning were giving me the look of, "I told you so."

Maybe it was because it was the Olympic year and the pressure was heavy. Maybe I was just having a dry spell. Maybe I was overthinking everything. Maybe I was letting the voices of the people who believed I wouldn't succeed affect me. I honestly don't know. What I do know is that I was on fire on the other five events, and on my best event, I couldn't get close to performing at an acceptable Olympic standard.

Coach and I had to make a tough decision. As we approached the games that year, I couldn't let one event out of the six ruin everything. We decided to take a few of the riskiest elements out of the routine to make sure I wouldn't fall. My pride took a hit! I was the national champion on high bar. I was known for those skills, and now I was having to remove them because I couldn't perform them properly.

But still, we arrived in Beijing, China for the Olympics, and it was an unbelievably surreal experience to represent the USA.

During the preliminary round of competition, I did my new watered-down high bar routine and nailed it about as well as I possibly could. Sure, it was great to do a solid and well-performed routine, but I felt so unsatisfied every time because I knew I had more to offer than the skills I had performed.

I'm not sure how I pulled it off, but after the preliminary round of competition, I was sitting in 7th place on high bar. Any athlete who finishes in the top eight on an event would get the opportunity to compete again in the medal round five days later.

I was shocked that I got into the top 8, and I starting formulating a crazy idea. Two things became very clear: 1. I would have no chance at a medal with my easier, safer routine, and 2. I could change my plan back to include the original, riskier skills, add a few new skills that I had never used before, and that may give me a shot at the podium. I'm sure you can see where this story is leading!

So, on the biggest stage of my career, I figured, "What the heck; I have nothing to lose."

I told my coach and my Olympic teammates about my plan. They all looked at me like I was insane.

Coach said, "Absolutely not. You're not going to try a brand-new routine at the Olympics. Nobody changes their routines last minute, and you don't want to look like a fool by falling on worldwide TV."

My teammates just laughed and told me that they would rather not see me die in front of a billion spectators. I smirked back at them, and I could see in their eyes that they were giddy with excitement to see what would happen.

With a few days between the prelims and high bar finals, I begged my coach to at least let me try the routine in our training sessions. I suspect he conceded just to keep me quiet.

I tried this radical routine roughly 7-10 times, and I splattered on my face, side, back, face again, and every other surface of my body over and over, and over again.

All the other gymnasts from China, Japan, Germany, Russia and others who were preparing for their final performances were just laughing. I could see it all over their faces, "who is this stupid American, and why is he trying to kill himself?"

I had this feeling in my soul that I could complete the routine. I also knew that doing the other one would guarantee me, at best, a 7th- or 8th- place finish. I wanted to know that I at least had a shot at gold.

There is a quote that was etched in my brain, and I couldn't get it out. My favorite quote from the movie, "*Miracle*," about the 1980 Men's Olympic Hockey team, is when the head coach, Herb Brooks, says, "If we played 'em ten times, they might win 9. But not this game. Not tonight."

Coach finally saw it in my eyes that I wanted it bad, and I got his support in the end. My teammates saw that this was no longer a game, and I was willing to risk a fall at the Olympics for the opportunity to be a champion.

I stood under the bar with my coach, the only athlete in the entire arena about to perform. The arena of 40,000 was electric, and I'll never forget the moment that the judges raised their hands to signal to me that they were ready. I raised my hand back to the judges, and my coach lifted me to the bar.

I began my routine with more adrenaline than I had ever felt, and I was flying around the bar at lightning speed. I released the bar for my first element, which was one I added just for that occasion. I stuck my hands out blindly and they wrapped perfectly around the steel bar. I couldn't believe I wasn't lying on the mats below. I had successfully completed the hardest element in the routine!

I released the bar a second time – same result. Then a third, and then a fourth. Every single time I flew over the bar, my body was placed in the perfect position to re-grab the apparatus and continue flawlessly.

I got to the end of my routine, and I could hear the crowd roaring with excitement. Typically, after so many difficult skills, my body would begin to break down with fatigue and my breathing would feel heavy, but at this moment, I wasn't even the slightest bit tired.

I wound up for my dismount. At the time, it was the hardest dismount being performed in the world. I let go of the bar and did a triple twisting double back flip. I landed securely on my feet, and at that very moment I became the second-best gymnast in the world.

Winning the silver medal may not be the ending you may have hoped for from this story, but I'll take silver over 7th any day. I *won* that silver medal that day and nobody can ever convince me that I lost the gold.

One of my favorite current athletes is José Altuve, second baseman for the Houston Astros. In a sport where most athletes are well over six feet tall, Altuve is 5' 6" and only 164 pounds.

When he was 16 years old, he attended a camp in his hometown in Venezuela. The scouts turned him away because he was too small, but his father told him to go back and try again. In spite of being turned away, Altuve was adamant that the scouts let him try out. As you may know, the scouts eventually gave him a shot. Twelve years later, Altuve is a World Series champion, six-time All-Star and MVP.

Almost every time Altuve steps up to the plate, he swings so hard at the first pitch it nearly knocks him off his feet. He's aggressive and goes all out when he plays, and I can see the chip on his shoulder at every single game. He's got something to prove, and he's not afraid to swing the bat. He's not afraid to take the shot and miss, and because of it, he's consistently one of the best players in major league baseball.

There are times in our lives when we will be up against great odds—odds so great that society will tell us that the obstacle ahead is impossible to overcome, regardless of our level of expertise. If there is one thing that I have learned from other great athletes, it's that they take the shot. They don't hold back. When the moment is the scariest, the idea of being tentative and timid never creeps into their minds. Sure, they get nervous. But the nerves are part of what makes the moment so great.

If you ever have the opportunity to go for the gold, take the game winning shot or sprint to the finish, go all out. Wouldn't you rather know that you gave it your all and risked failure than be plagued with the "what if's" that come with choosing to play it safe?

Famous hockey player, Wayne Gretzky said it best, "You miss 100% of the shots you don't take."

Go for it. Take the shot.

Chapter 17

THE CHAMPION'S TRAP

In 2006, I experienced one of the most humiliating moments of my life.

I led the US men's team to the worst performance in the history of USA gymnastics. I fell six times across six different apparatus, and the team finished in 13th place because of my mistakes.

I was a 20-year-old sophomore in college and supposedly an up and coming star for the sport in America. My career had finally taken off after so many years of coming up short. Just before college, I had been a Junior National Champion, the youngest gymnast in the country to qualify for the Olympic trials in 2004, and one of the few to receive a full scholarship to school.

I felt like I had arrived, and I was one of the best. I was ready to not only prove myself on the world stage, but the Olympic stage.

So, in 2006, I qualified to compete on my very first World Championships team. In gymnastics, the World Team is a big deal. It's basically as big of a competition as the Olympics, but since the Olympics are every four years, the sport hosts a World Championship each of the other three years. Only six gymnasts had the honor of wearing the red, white, and blue with USA on our uniforms, and I was one of them.

I was pumped! The problem that I would later discover, however, was that I thought the work had already been done. I became arrogant and overconfident. I had helped Oklahoma win the national title the year before, and in my mind, the only things left to check off my list were World medals and Olympic medals.

I remember telling the team how excited I was that we were going to Worlds. I had this big dream of becoming a first-time World Champion with multiple medals around my neck and people shouting my name from the bleachers. I was able to see so clearly an image of myself on top of the awards podium with my teammates at my side and the American flag in the air.

None of that happened.

I was the lead-off man on the very first event, which was the floor exercise. I remember walking into the arena which was packed with excited fans. I had never competed in front of more than a few hundred people, but this arena had thousands. There were men with cameras throughout, eight judges sitting by each event, and every apparatus was cream- and red-colored, which was weird since I was used to blue and white.

I stepped up to the first event with confidence. The floor was one of my best events. I was the current national champion on floor and I rarely made mistakes. I nodded over to my teammates to let them know, "I got this," and I took off for my performance.

I had five intricate tumbling runs in my routine; each of them with different flipping and twisting elements and degrees of difficulty. I was flying through my routine with ease until I approached my dismount, which was a full-twisting double back flip. I had been performing the skill for many years already, and it was a given that I would have no problem completing it successfully.

Just as I was about to start running for the final skill, I froze in the corner of the forty-foot by forty-foot floor. My legs were shaking, and my heart sunk with a nervousness I had never experienced. I took a second to take an extra breath and forced myself to run in spite of what my body felt like it could do. I jumped in the air to do the skill with one full 360° twist and two flips, met the ground with my feet, and fell to my butt.

My first World Championship performance was a bust, and I didn't improve on it much during my five other routines. My teammates tried to keep me encouraged, event after event, but I lost my confidence more and more after every blunder. Six falls later, not only did the team place in its worst position ever, but no other gymnast from USA had ever fallen as many times as I did at a major international competition.

I let Team USA down in an epic way that hasn't been repeated since. I was supposed to be the savior, the new kid on the block who had everything going for him, but I wasn't.

I went through a very mentally taxing time after that competition. I told myself that I wouldn't ever pursue elite world competitions again. I barely wanted to finish competing for my school, and for a while I wanted to quit. I was the biggest mistake the selection committee had ever made for an international team. My teammates, coaches and fans were furious with me. I was furious with me, too.

My experience at the World Championships in 2006 was indisputably the most important moment in my entire career. Because of that experience, I realized that I had let off the gas pedal. When I did, I crashed hard. I like to say that I fell into "The Champion's Trap."

For those of us who are fortunate enough to experience big time success, complacency can become a major temptation. I know beyond a shadow of a doubt that I stopped training as hard. I wasn't as focused. My coaches and teammates didn't seem as important anymore, and I started to stray from being a good teammate. At that moment, I had worked for 16 years to be one of the greatest. My work ethic and passion had driven me to become one of the best, but one moment stripped everything away, and the sport lost its trust in me.

I eventually pulled myself out of the hole that I dug for myself, but it came after a lot of tears, frustration, heartache and a deep search of my soul. But I desperately wanted to prove myself to my team, country, and coaches.

So if you're reading this, remember: never let up. Keep moving forward at every level. I don't care if you are in the beginning stages of your sport or career or one of the greatest of all time. Put the pedal to the metal and work to be better. You don't want to get caught in the trap of feeling like the work is done.

It only takes one moment of belief that we are good enough and no longer need the same effort, to create a moment of failure as catastrophic as mine. I promise, you do not want to let your team down. Be the leader who always keeps pushing the limits.

In a way, I'm thankful for what happened to me. I'm not okay with what I did to my team, but on a personal level I know that this was the greatest learning experience of my 30 years in the sport. Without this moment, I don't know if I would have continued to advance the way I did. The lessons I learned from being the biggest disaster the sport has seen drove me to a higher level, but I still wish there had been a better path to success that didn't involve imploding on the world stage. If only I had known that the work is never finished, maybe I wouldn't still have the sour taste in my mouth from the 2006 World Championships.

I hope you don't get caught in The Champion's Trap like I did, but if you ever find yourself there, congratulations. You now know how badly it hurts. You're angry. You're sad. But you're going to use this moment to drive you into your greatest season, and you're not going to let this happen again.

Chapter 18

SPORTS DON'T LAST FOREVER

W hen I was a young kid, there was nothing that I loved more than doing gymnastics and having the opportunity to compete. I knew for a fact that I would be able to do my sport longer than anyone, and I felt like I was invincible.

I was almost right, but reality set in during my late twenties. I always felt like I was bulletproof. I never thought that my body would break down. I was a little bit lucky, too—I didn't suffer a major injury until I was 26 years old!

All that changed during competition at the World Championships in 2011. I did a relatively new, complicated vault, and the result was a terrible landing that destroyed my left foot. I broke two bones and tore a ligament called the Lisfranc. After surgeries and screws, it took me nine months to return to full strength.

Unfortunately, my injuries seemed to snowball from that moment. The next year I had to have a major reconstructive surgery on my right shoulder. After a year of intense physical therapy to come back, I tore my pectoral muscle in my first competition post-surgery. Then, nine months before the 2016 Olympics, I needed surgery to completely reconstruct my left shoulder.

It felt like it happened out of the blue, but suddenly I was always hurt and not performing up to elite standards. When I turned 32, the time came to finally throw in the towel.

It was a tough day, and one that I never imagined coming. It came abruptly, and it was brutal. The hardest part was realizing how much of my identity was rooted in my athleticism. When I realized I wouldn't get to compete again, I experienced one of the most emotional times in my life. Not only did I not have a shot at being in the Olympics again, but I was also injured and unable to really do anything while recovering. This became problematic!

In the blink of an eye, I had gone from being a successful professional athlete, to someone who was trying to find my new identity as a person, recover from an injury, and find a way to survive financially.

When I look back on my career as a gymnast, the education that I have, and my time spent on everything else, I wish that I'd had my reality check ten years earlier. Had it struck me sooner that the day would come that I would no longer be a professional athlete, I think the transition would have been a little simpler.

Planning for the future is essential, and it will really help with the anxiety and stress of transitioning from being an athlete to a more traditional work life.

In the latter part of my gymnastics career, things were great. I trained in the mornings, I trained in the afternoon, and then I went home and spent time with my wife. I made good money as a pro athlete. I had tons of free time after I was done training. I used to go home and play video games or go out to dinner and a movie with my wife. No one sat me down to say, "Hey, Jonathan, what are you doing NOW to prepare for when you aren't doing gymnastics anymore?"

I always assumed that I would have an easy transition into something lucrative and a great opportunity would just fall into my lap. So, my answer to the question may have been, "Nothing, I'm good."

When I finished gymnastics, I had zero income, no health insurance, and I was married with two children. Not having a plan is one of the most irresponsible things I ever did in my life. I experienced stress and anxiety for several years unlike anything before. I watched the money that I made disappear, and at one point, I was desperate to make something work.

Okay, maybe not "desperate." I wasn't ever begging for money, but I was begging for opportunity. I had always had in the back of my mind that I wanted to be a motivational speaker, and as I started pursuing that dream, I found that just like anything else, it takes a lot of time, work ethic and patience to be a high-demand speaker.

If I could go back in time, I would make a list of my strengths and weaknesses, what I love to do (and what I don't love to do), and how I feel that I can best serve people. I would take my list and find a way to start developing a career that would be sustainable after my competitive career ended.

There are opportunities out there for you right now, but you must be willing to put some time toward your future - every single day. Athletes who are in college, or professionals who are blessed enough to make a living from their sports, should all be looking for these opportunities while they are still competing and playing. Let's hedge against an uncertain future.

Here are some ideas to tinker with that could become lucrative over time, and won't be a distraction from your full-time training or career:

- Find a good and reputable home-based network marketing business
- Start a blog
- Write a book
- Get involved with speaking clubs to see if motivational speaking excites you
- Create an online training program
- Get a real estate license.

Every single one of those options can be done on your own time, and you can build those careers as slow or fast and as big or small as you choose.

In my time of struggle, I found several different opportunities that I had to fully commit to in order to make ends meet. I certainly learned a lot along the way as well, and I eventually began to see the fruits of my labor. My only wish is that I had started sooner.

In reality, we all want to be Tiger Woods, Lebron James, or Tom Brady and make millions of dollars, but the odds are against us. Maybe some of us can be great at our sports and do well, but the truth is that most of us will need to prepare for our financial future beyond elite sports.

As much as you love it, your athletic careers won't last forever. With a little extra time and dedication each day, however, you can make the transition into the real world a lot easier on yourself.

FINAL THOUGHTS

I've been blessed to accomplish some amazing things in my time as an elite athlete; Junior National Champion, Senior National Champion, multiple World Cup titles, World team member and medalist, and multiple-time Olympic medalist. It's a little strange, but I even get to call myself a professional ninja!

I don't list the above to brag or to boast about my life, but simply to make one point: It's not how you start, it's how you finish.

I wasn't the most talented kid in the world, but what I lacked in talent I made up for in work ethic and passion. In the end, those basic traits were the most important to my success.

I wanted to be an Olympian so badly I couldn't stand it, regardless of what anyone told me. I knew it was possible, but I was going to have to do things the more talented athletes didn't need to worry about.

I do want to take a moment to address one topic I just mentioned: passion. I was an extremely passionate athlete. I discovered what I wanted to do at a young age, and I was 100% committed to my goal without ever wavering. Sure, I had moments I thought quitting would be easier, but in my heart, I knew I couldn't do it because I was too passionate about becoming an Olympian.

I used to tell people when they asked me about how to be motivated that they needed to find a goal or a passion that they simply couldn't live without, and if they found it, it would be impossible to ever quit the mission.

Recently, my beliefs about passion were challenged in a big way. I had someone reach out to me and say, "Watch this." It was a video of Elizabeth Gilbert, the author of **Eat, Pray, Love** speaking on stage about passion. Liz, who is an extremely accomplished author and speaker, discusses how she used to speak to crowds about how they need to find their passion, and that the only way to succeed was to be passionate; passion, passion, passion. This was her message until someone wrote her a long email about how they were in a worse place in their life after listening to one of her motivational speeches. This individual had tried their entire life to find a passion, but she was unsuccessful, and therefore felt like a failure and a loser.

Liz goes on to talk about how the bottom dropped out of her core belief system, and that she discovered that it's okay to not be hugely passionate about something. In her words, some of us are like jackhammers. We find one thing to focus on, and we hammer at it until the job is done. Others of us, however, are hummingbirds. We fly from one thing to another but live beautiful and loving lives.

As I write this book, I want to make sure that I don't leave out those hummingbirds. We all have different interests, skills, work ethics, and passions. If you aren't like me and didn't discover your one passion at a young age, that's okay! Here's what I want to leave you with: If you identify more with the hummingbird, open every single door of opportunity that comes your way, and don't stress out if you can't find what you want to pour all of your heart and soul into. Every single opportunity that comes is one that you should consider looking into, no matter how ordinary or extraordinary it may seem. Be bold and try new things every day. Scare yourself and try something you thought you wouldn't ever do because you never know if you'll discover a hidden love for it.

If you can't find your passion, I want you to know that you aren't weird, and you certainly aren't destined to fail. Honestly, I think you may be the majority. I'll be transparent with my beliefs, though, and tell you something that Elizabeth Gilbert didn't—by discovering your passion and committing to it, I believe you give yourself a better chance to live an extraordinary life. So many people never find one thing to commit to, and instead of becoming great at one thing, they are just good at a few things. I'm not saying you can't live a big life without finding your passion, but I do think it will be harder. A lot of people in this world live tremendous lives and they aren't sure what they really love to do, but I think your life deserves a relentless and unwavering search for your passion.

I found out what my passion was, and I loved it, but it came at a cost. I wasn't the cool kid in school. I was the lame, short kid who flipped, somersaulted, and wore goofy tight outfits to try and impress judges. I had to listen to a lot of people tell me that my sport wasn't a sport, the uniforms we wore were stupid, and that gymnastics was only a women's sport. It wasn't always easy, but I knew that what I wanted was more important than trying to impress the people who were putting me down.

I loved every moment of my time as a gymnast; the good and the bad. And the bad was worth it because I loved standing on top of an awards podium after competition. Trust me, there isn't anything quite like having an Olympic medal placed around your neck. The moment passes by quickly, but those few minutes brought me more joy than I could have ever imagined.

Although it may not make too much sense to some of you, in hindsight, I even loved the moments of failure. The competitions where I finished in last place, the days in the gym when I fell on every routine, and even the day I led Team USA to the worst performance in the history of the sport, were some of the most powerful experiences of my career. Without them I wouldn't have had the success I did as an athlete.

Throughout my career, I had to force myself to make sacrifices for something that I wasn't even sure would pan out in the end. I sacrificed time with friends, family, vacations, college parties, delicious fatty food, desserts, and anything else I thought might hinder my chances. But I knew that if I didn't make all of those sacrifices, I would live with regret in the end for not doing everything I could to achieve my goals.

I've written this book because 'If I Had Known' more when I was younger, I might've been able to side-step some of the painful bumps and bruises I experienced along the way. What I have now is the benefit of 20/20 hindsight from a professional career. The many lessons, both small and large, that I learned along the way taught me what it takes to succeed. If this book helps even one person avoid some of the pitfalls I experienced, then I believe this story will have been worth sharing. Maybe that person is you!

Whether you're an aspiring professional athlete, an up and coming entrepreneur or have other ambitious goals altogether, here's what I want you to take from my story:

Your journey won't last forever, so risk it all and give your dream everything you have.

If you have a dream, go all out. Make the decision early on that no matter what, you won't quit. Exhaust every resource you can to make that dream a reality. Fight until the bitter end and find something valuable to take away from every situation, not just in competition, but every single day as you inch closer and closer to the goal. Forget what people say about you, forget about the obstacles that may lie ahead, and focus on your dream.

Our dreams are the one thing that nobody can take from us. The only person who can give up on your goal is you! Right now – make the decision to be great. It will probably take a while to get where you want to go, so embrace every part of your journey.

Good luck.

I believe in you.

Made in the USA
San Bernardino, CA
15 January 2019